The 7 Day

Stress
Buster

J. Alexander

First published in Great Britain in 2007 by Hodder Children's Books

Text copyright © Jenny Alexander 2007
Illustration copyright © David Whittle 2007
Design by Don Martin

The rights of Jenny Alexander and David Whittle to be identified as
the Author and Illustrator of this Work have been asserted by them
in accordance with the Copyright, Designs and Patents Act 1988.

1

A catalogue record for this book is available from the British Library.

ISBN-13: 978 0 340 93068 7

Printed and bound by Bookmarque Ltd, Croydon, Surrey

The paper and board used in this paperback by Hodder Children's Books are
natural recyclable products made from wood grown in sustainable forests. The
manufacturing processes conform to the environmental regulations of the
country of origin.

Hodder Children's Books
A division of Hachette Children's Books
338 Euston Road, London NW1 3BH

CONTENTS

Other titles in the Seven Day series:

The Seven Day Self Esteem Super-Booster
The Seven Day Brain Booster
The Seven Day Bully Buster

INTRODUCTION

About stress

In the olden days, your biggest health worry would have been that you might die of boredom ...

But these days, there's always loads to do and the problem isn't boredom so much as stress ...

Just about every part of life is more stressy now than it used to be. For example:

● School – you've got more tests than ever before, more homework and less fun stuff in the curriculum, like sport, drama, singing, art, cooking, crafts and music.

● Family – most mums and dads work longer hours than they used to, and that can make them feel tired and tetchy, which rubs off on everyone else.

- Friends – there's no time out because MSN and mobile messaging means you can be in touch 24:7.

- Looking good – you get big pressure to have the right clothes and be the right shape, mostly from TV and magazines.

- Having the right stuff – this wasn't an issue in the old days because no one had much money and there wasn't much stuff to buy.

- The state of the world – we've got round-the-clock media coverage of everything bad that ever happens, whipping up panic about global warming, crime, terrorism, hedgehog flu etc.

Life is super-speed compared to the olden days, too. People don't walk or cycle much – it's all cars, trains, buses and planes, whizzing us around all over the place. And everything's instant, from messaging to remote control TV and music at the touch of a button.

Not many people would want to go back to the boring old days and most of the time everything feels fine. A little bit of stress is actually good for you – it keeps you on your toes, helps you do your best and makes you feel alive. But sometimes

INTRODUCTION

busy, busy, busy all the time can get to be a bit much. You can start feeling stressed – and then even small setbacks can seem like huge problems, and you can find it hard to cope.

It's like the proverbial camel being loaded up with straw – he can take an awful lot, but there's a limit, and if no one notices that he's buckling under the pressure, the last straw can break the camel's back.

Are you feeling under too much pressure? Check out to see if you need to do something about it by doing the 'last straw' tick test.

The last-straw tick test

Here are 12 possible signs of stress. Give one tick to any that happen to you sometimes, two ticks to any that happen a lot, and no ticks to any that never happen at all.

Getting tetchy over nothing ☐

Stressing over schoolwork ☐

Thinking your head's going to explode ☐

Having accidents ☐

Breaking / losing things ☐

Refusing to get out of bed ☐

Lying awake worrying ☐

Losing your temper ☐

Tummy ache / headache ☐

Bursting into tears ☐

Falling out with friends ☐

Fretting about family stuff ☐

Results

Add up all your ticks. If you had …

More than 12 You're stressed out – you need to start stress-busting right now before your camel keels over.

6–11 You're a bit stressed – start stress-busting to stop it getting worse.

1–5 You're pretty laid back – but you might as well read on, since you've got all the time in the world.

None at all Might be worth checking for a pulse!

The art of stress-busting

The best way to deal with stress is to take a holiday. 'Pah!' I hear you say, 'That's all very well, but what if you haven't got any money and your parents can't take time off work and it's term time anyway so you just can't go away?'

Woah, there – keep your wig on! I didn't say you have to have three weeks on a tropical beach whenever you feel a touch of tetchiness coming on. You can get all the benefits of a great holiday in the comfort of your own home, without going anywhere at all.

A holiday has seven great stress-busting benefits –

 1 Leaving your worries behind

 2 Getting back to nature

 3 Letting your hair down

 4 Having a laugh

 5 Pampering yourself

 6 Doing some physical activity

 7 Having a change of scene

INTRODUCTION

By a happy coincidence, there are also seven days in a week, and that brings me to the beauty of this book.

About this book

There are seven chapters in this book – one for each day of the week – and each chapter covers one of the seven stress-busting benefits of going on holiday. All you have to do is read a chapter a day and pick something from the 'Choice of mini-breaks' at the end.

It's as easy as ABC –

A Before you go to bed, read the chapter for the following day and decide which mini-break you're going to do.

B When you get up in the morning, remind yourself what it is.

C Some time during the day, do it!

Note: It's best to start on a Sunday evening, so if you're reading this on a Wednesday, sorry – you're just going to have to wait!

The 'seven day' system

You can feel the benefits of stress-busting in just one week, so it can be a quick fix if you're feeling really stressy. But to get the most out of it, you need to turn it into a habit – if stress-busting's part of your everyday life you're much less likely to get stressed out in the first place. If you want to get the habit, when you get to Sunday you simply start all over again, choosing different mini-breaks.

You won't have to re-read the chapters if you don't feel like it because they're very short and you'll be able to remember what's in them. You can just choose your mini-break for each day and do it.

There are enough mini-breaks for a different one every day for ten weeks.

Two top stress-busting tips

1 Have a go at as many different mini-breaks as you can, but skip any that really don't appeal to you – enjoyment is the key to success.

2 Try not to miss a day. It's much better to do a mini-break – even one you've done before – than nothing at all.

One week will make a difference, two weeks will make twice the difference – the longer you keep it up, the calmer and happier you will feel.

Ten treats for ten weeks

If you decide to try for the full ten weeks give yourself a little incentive. Every Sunday, buy a small treat and wrap it up like a present. Put it somewhere safe.

If you're doing the stress-buster with a mate, buy a little gift for each other or if you've got the sort of mum / dad / grandma / grandpa / friend who likes helping, ask them to do it for you.

At the end of ten weeks stress-busting it'll be like Christmas – you'll have ten lovely treats to unwrap and enjoy!

The seven-day system is brilliant because –

- **It's easy**
  The mini-breaks only take a few minutes each day, but simply thinking about them takes your mind off your worries.

- **It's fun**
  A little holiday every day – need I say more?

- **It's good for you, your family and friends**
  Too much stress can damage your health and happiness, make you less likely to succeed and play havoc with your relationships. You'll be less snappy and more fun, and your laid-backness will rub off on the people around you and help them to feel more relaxed themselves.

The seven-day stress-busting club

The seven-day approach is very flexible. You can do it by yourself if you like doing things on your own, but it's also great to share with other people.

You can enjoy the mini-breaks with your best mate or a group of friends, and compare notes afterwards. You can do them with your mum or dad if you're in a family that likes doing things together. You can ask your teacher to start a seven-day stress-busting set at school.

It doesn't matter how you do it, as soon as you start you'll be part of the global seven day stress-busting club because everyone who's got this book, wherever they are in the world, will be choosing from the same choice of mini-breaks on the same day as you. Imagine!

Ready, steady ... reminder time

Unless you happen to be reading this on a Sunday evening, it's time to close the book now. Leave yourself a reminder to start on Sunday somewhere you can't miss it – on your mobile, say, or a note beside the bed.

Ttfn! *

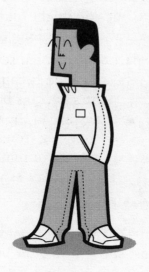

*Ta ta for now

INTRODUCTION

I said, close the book! Still, I knew you wouldn't, and actually there are a few things you could do before lift-off time on Sunday.

1 Get a special note pad

This will be a nice private place to do any mini-breaks that involve a bit of writing or drawing, plus you can use it like a journal to jot down your own ideas and comments and chart your progress, stress-wise. Only do it if you want to, but you might find it's actually a really relaxing way of winding down at the end of the day.

Your special note pad is like a diary – you might show it to some people but you wouldn't want the whole world and his dog to see it, so ...

2 Find a secret hiding place

Not for you – for your note pad! Don't be slack and just shove it in your undies drawer – that's so unimaginative and besides, your mum would find it the very next time she tried to track down all the odd socks.

3 Make a record sheet

This is just for people who either like keeping record sheets or won't be able to remember which tasks they've done without one.

You could do it at the back of your special note pad if you've got one.

	Mon	Tues	Wed	Thurs	Fri	Sat	Sun
Week 1	5	2	10	4	2	7	6
2							
3							
4							
5							
6							
7							
8							
9							
10							

4 Think about getting some stress-buster buddies

If you decide someone you know might want to join in, get them on board now before you begin.

I think that just about does it, so now you really must close the book until Sunday evening, OK? I mean it!

1 MONDAY

Leave your worries behind

The biggest cause of stress is worries. Worries weigh you down, and you can't get a good break if you're lugging a whole lot of extra weight around with you.

You need some worries in life just like you need some luggage when you go on holiday – a toothbrush and some spare socks, for example – but if you're feeling stressed then you're probably carrying a lot more than you need.

Worries come in two different varieties

- Silly worries
- Sensible worries

Fortunately, most worries are completely nuts and as soon as you spot they're silly you can simply let them go. Phew! That feels better!

Spotting the silly ones

Whenever you feel worried about something, ask yourself the golden question – 'Is there anything I can do about it?'

Worrying about things you can't do anything about makes as much sense as lugging your snowsuit and skis around with you on a trip to the Sahara.

Do 'The worry-sorter tick test' and see if you can sort out the silly worries from the sensible ones.

The worry-sorter tick test

Look at these common worries and ask yourself, 'Is there anything I can do about it?' Then put a tick beside the sensible ones and a cross beside the silly ones.

1 I might get run over ☐

2 I might be blown up by terrorists ☐

3 I might fall out with my friends ☐

4 I might get a big spot on my nose ☐

5 We might have to move house ☐

6 Mum and dad might have a
   big row ☐

7 I might get the flesh-eating
   bug/mad cow disease/bird flu ☐

8 I might miss the school bus ☐

9 I might fail my maths test ☐

10 The earth might get blasted to
   bits by an asteroid ☐

Answers

Tick   1, 3, 8 and 9 are all sensible worries because you can do something about them – look before you cross, be a good friend yourself, get up early enough and do some revision.

Cross   2, 4, 5, 6, 7 and 10 are all silly things to worry about because you can't do anything to prevent them happening. You getting your knickers in a knot won't make them any less likely – it'll just make you feel miserable.

Once you spot that something you're worrying about is actually a silly worry, you can just let go of it. But what about the sensible ones?

Sensible worries

Sensible worries serve a purpose – they either keep you safe or help you to be more effective in your life – so you wouldn't want to just forget about them.

I mean, supposing you decided not to worry about getting lost? You could wander off any-old-where and spend three hours trying to find your way back home.

Supposing you had a part in the school panto and you decided not to worry about forgetting your lines? You wouldn't bother to rehearse and then the next thing you know you're up on stage, as red as a beetroot, with everyone staring at you and no idea at all what you're supposed to be saying. Nightmare!

But it's no good just holding on to sensible worries – you have to actually do something about them. Otherwise, you can end up stressing out, like Courtney.

Courtney

When Courtney started in a new school, her new friends invited her to go ice-skating with them. She really wanted to go but she was scared of making a fool of herself.

This was a perfectly sensible worry, given that Courtney had never been ice-skating before in her life and there was something she could do about it. She could have got her mum to take her for a practice before the day, or she could have 'fessed up that she'd never been before, so the other girls wouldn't expect her to be as good as them.

But Courtney didn't do anything – she stressed. She spent all week thinking would she/wouldn't she go. She lost sleep over it. She got into a state. In the end, she bottled out at the last minute, which made her new friends annoyed and meant she ended up feeling like a loser.

When it comes to sensible worries, here's a good plan –

First ...

Don't panic.

Use some simple relaxation techniques to help you keep calm (check these out in the Menu of Monday mini-breaks).

Second ...

Work out what you can do.

Be realistic and remember that doing something small is better than doing nothing at all – for example, a taster session with her mum would have been better than nothing for Courtney, even though she didn't have time for a complete professional ice-skating course.

Third ...

Do it!

It usually helps to set a timetable of some sort. Say you're trying for the netball team, half an hour a day shooting hoops and ten minutes fitness training might be a good schedule.

So here you have it, the first rule of stress-busting – travel light. Check through all the worries that might be stressing you out, and ditch the silly ones.

Make sure the only things you let yourself feel worried about are ones you can do something about – and then get on and do it!

Start sorting out your worries now by choosing a Monday mini-break.

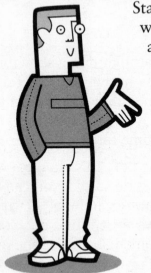

Menu of Monday mini-breaks

❶ A problem shared ...

... is a problem halved, as they say. One way of lightening the load is by talking about your worries with someone you trust. Write a list of five people you could talk to if you felt really worried about something.

If you feel really worried about something right now, try talking to one of them.

❷ The worry box

Get a small box – a matchbox would be ideal. Use paint or felt tip pen to colour it black, or cover it with black paper. This is your worry box.

When you go to bed at night, write down anything you feel worried about on a scrap of paper and put it in the box. This is a great way of putting your worries aside so that you can go to sleep and not lie awake fretting – which is pointless because however sensible your worry is, there's nothing you can do about it in the middle of the night.

Your worry will still be there when you wake up if you want to start thinking about it again, though usually in the morning things don't look quite so bad.

❸ Breathe in, breathe out!

If you feel worried you can stop yourself getting in a panic by simply taking notice of your breathing. This is a variation on the breathe-into-a-paper-bag technique that works when someone's hyperventilating (breathing so fast they might pass out).

Whenever you feel angry, anxious or agitated today, notice your breathing and see how that calms you down. It's as simple as that – breathe in ... breathe out!

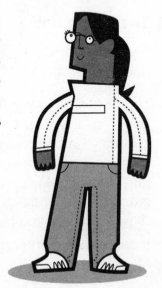

❹ Be your own agony aunt

Think of something you tend to worry about – one of those worries you come back to even if it isn't at the forefront of your mind right now.

Pretend you're an agony aunt on your fave magazine and write yourself a letter about it. E.g.: 'Dear *(your own name)*, Whenever I get a tummy ache I think I might be really ill ...'

Then write an answer to yourself, saying what you think an agony aunt would say. 'Dear Shaz, It probably isn't anything to worry about because it seems to have happened lots of times and always just got better. Still, maybe you could talk to your mum or dad about it next time cos a problem shared is a problem halved, as they say ...'

❺ Soothe yourself to sleep

Worries sometimes stop you getting to sleep because even mad ones can seem quite sensible when you're lying there in the dark.

Have a really soothing bedtime by

- Having a glass of hot milk
- Eating a banana or a handful of peanuts
- Winding down with ten minutes reading, all snuggled up in bed

Milk, bananas and peanuts are foods that make you feel sleepy – that's a scientific fact. And unlike watching TV, reading doesn't make your brain go into over-drive – unless it's a really scary story!

❻ Do a reality check

List five things you sometimes worry about. Go through them one by one, asking yourself, 'Is there anything I can do?'

If the answer to any of them is no, decide to let them go. Then next time one of them comes up, you'll remember and think, 'No. I've dealt with that.'

❼ Zoom out

Most of the time, we're completely focused on a very small area – say a TV screen or a book – and we don't even notice what's going on at the edge of our vision.

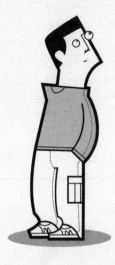

Once in the morning, once in the afternoon and once in the evening, take a few moments to zoom out. Keep looking at whatever you're focused on but try to become aware of what you can see all around you without moving your eyes. Use your other senses to become aware of things going on behind you too.

This has a very interesting effect. It slows everything down. You can use it any time you feel a bit stressy. How great is that?

❽ Wipe off your whiteboard

Sit quietly and shut your eyes. Take a few slow, deep breaths to help you concentrate your mind.

Now imagine a whiteboard with a choice of coloured markers. Imagine choosing a marker, and write on the whiteboard anything you feel worried about, for example

not being able to do my maths

Write it clearly and slowly, and then stand back to look at it. Take a cloth and wipe it clean. If you still feel worried, write it again and wipe it off again. Write and wipe as many times as you like – it feels so good!

If another worry pops into your head as you're doing this, write and wipe that one as well.

❾ Find your centre

Close your eyes and imagine a spot just below your belly button, half way between the back of your body and the front. This is your point of power. The Japanese Samurai warriors practised focusing on this point because it's a way of feeling strong and stopping anxious thoughts.

Mark a dot on your thumbnail and every time you notice it, remember your point of power.

⑩ Make a plan

Think of a sensible worry you've got and write down a sensible plan of action. For example, maybe you're worried about global warming. Well, you can't save the planet all on your own, but you could do your bit by:

- Remembering to turn off lights you aren't using.

- Switching the TV off at the set instead of leaving it on stand-by.

- Unplugging your charger as soon as your mobile phone is fully charged.

Or maybe you're worried about something closer to home.

I'm worried about getting my new phone pinched.

Plan –

> Put it on mute and don't answer it
> when I'm walking along the road or on
> public transport.
> Don't leave my bag around at school
> if my phone's in it.

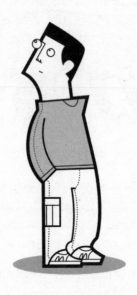

2 TUESDAY

Go back to nature

Most holidays involve going to the coast
or countryside and getting closer to nature.
That's because nature is slow and quiet –
the opposite of most people's normal lives.

Have you noticed that when adults ask
each other 'How are you?', the answer is
nearly always something like 'I'm very
busy' – as if being busy is more important
than health and happiness. Being busy is
so normal that if you aren't actually doing
anything there's a good chance your mum

or dad might think there's something wrong
with you.

It's great to have lots to do all the time, with TVs
and computers and phones and MP3 players and
dance classes and music practices and extra
lessons and homework and whatever else you do
in your spare time ... but it can also be stressful.

You don't need to stop everything and turn into a
cabbage, but you do need to slow down
sometimes and give yourself a rest. See if you're
getting enough down-time by doing the 'Do you
really need to chill?' quiz.

Do you really need to chill?

Tick one thing in each section that most applies to you.

1 The first thing I do when I get in from school is

A Switch on the TV/computer.

B Stretch out and have a snooze/listen to music.

C Get ready for my sports practice/drama class/extra maths etc.

2 When I'm with my mates we mostly

A Play computer games.

B Just hang out.

C I'm too busy to have mates.

3 The best cure for boredom is

A The Simpsons.

B Having a kick-around / writing my diary / making something / chatting to a mate.

C No idea – I never get bored.

4 If I'm mooching around my mum / dad

A Suggests a DVD.

B Makes some tea and mooches too.

C Tells me to tidy my room / do some homework.

5 The last thing I do at night is

A Watch TV in my room.

B Curl up with the cat / dog / a good book.

C Fall asleep over my homework.

Results

Mostly A   A bit of TV can be great, but too much screen time over-stimulates the brain. You don't just need to chill – you need to get a life!

Mostly B   You're super-cool. Remember to rev up between relaxations and get a few things done.

Mostly C   Ooh ... stressy! Reorganise your timetable and make space for the Stress-buster.

Being busy 24:7 is stressful because it isn't natural. People are part of nature like all the other animals, and they can get worn out if they're on the go all the time. It's like the robins in built-up areas: they are fooled by street lights into thinking it's day, so they tweet away all night long and get completely exhausted.

So for a natural de-stress sometimes it's good to stop, switch off and see what happens.

Three things that happen when you stop and switch off

1 *Your body relaxes*

Aah … that feels good.

2 *You get an energy boost*

Some big businesses are experimenting with having snooze rooms as well as offices (this is true!) or having hammocks on hand for workers to lie around in whenever they feel like it – and the result? It looks as if, in some jobs, people actually work better if they have lots of ten minute rests.

I wonder if your teacher might go for this idea? Could be worth a try!

3 *Your life suddenly gets more interesting*

If you rush around all the time, or fill every waking moment with TV and computer games, your life gets more rigid and narrow, because there's simply no room for anything new and exciting to come in.

'Nature abhors a vacuum' as the boffins tell us – create a space and something is bound to come and fill it.

James

James normally spent the whole of every evening playing games on the computer, writing his blog and chatting to his mates in MSN. He got so engrossed in it that he never wanted to log off and go to bed, so every night ended with a big row between him and his dad. Finally, the inevitable happened – his dad banned him from using the computer for a week. Ouch!

For the first few days, James put most of his energy into having a major sulk but it was no good – however horrible he was, his parents wouldn't budge.

For the next few days, he sat around in his bedroom feeling bored out of his brain, flicking from one boring TV programme to another, reading bits of one boring book after another.

Then he went through his cupboard looking for something to do. He found the guitar his gran had bought him a few Christmases before that he'd never really bothered with. He sat on his bed and passed half an hour just randomly playing around with it.

By the end of the week, James had signed up for some guitar lessons. After a few months, he had joined a band. He didn't have so much time for the computer any more – he was too busy.

And the moral is? Don't underestimate the benefits of boredom!

Reconnecting with nature

The natural world is slow compared with the speed of human inventions like cars and instant messaging. It has rhythms of growth and rest – day and night; spring, summer, autumn and winter – unlike the continuous stimulation of TV and technology. That's why being in a natural environment is so relaxing when you're on holiday.

But you don't have to go to the coast or countryside in order to reconnect with nature – it's all around you. All you have to do is notice it. Five or ten minutes of noticing and appreciating nature is like a little holiday every day – and it's free.

So stop and smell the roses! Choose your Tuesday mini-break right now.

Menu of Tuesday mini-breaks

❶ Have a noticing nature walk

This is soooo easy. Most probably, you walk somewhere every day anyway, say to the shops, or school, or your mate's house, and in that case, it's just a question of noticing all the natural things you see as you go along.

For example – a cloud in the sky, a dog on a lead, a tree in a garden, flowers outside the fruit-and-veg shop ... Birds, earth, insects, rain ...

You'll be amazed how much you never usually notice.

❷ Do some holiday reading

Reading is very restful. You can go at your own natural pace and stop whenever you like – no crashing through the story between adverts. It's also silent and private (for anyone over about seven).

If you're bored with your usual favourites, go to the local library and choose something new for you – it might be an adult non-fiction book about football, for example, or a little-kid story that'll be sweet and easy to read.

Or check out the comics and puzzle books at your corner shop. It's all great when it's just you and the open page.

❸ Hug a tree!

This isn't as embarrassing as it sounds because there's no need to full-on hug it. In fact, it works just as well if you lean your back against the trunk and just sit or stand there for a while.

Look up into the branches and think about how long the tree has been growing – since before you were even born. Think about all the animals and birds that have made their home in it over the years.

❹ Feed the birds

When you were little your mum and dad might have taken you to feed the ducks, and probably those crackers quackers snatched the whole slice of bread out of your titchy mitts and frightened you to bits. Don't let that put you off!

Take an old crust, break it up and scatter the crumbs on your lawn / balcony / window sill. Then sit a little way away and wait for the birds to come.

❺ Cuddle up with the cat

Pets are great at getting people to relax. Doctors have found that stroking an animal actually brings your blood pressure down – unless of course it's next door's snarling pitbull.

Spend five minutes just stroking and talking to your pet today – if you haven't got one, arrange to visit someone else's.

❻ Make friends with fruit

Fresh fruit is nature you can eat! Take two or three different types of fruit – for example, an apple, some grapes and a banana – and be creative. You might:

● Peel and chop them up and pour some fruit juice over them to make a fresh fruit salad.

● Peel, chop and pop them in a blender with some water or yoghurt to make a delicious fruit smoothie.

● Slice them up and arrange the slices on a big plate around a pot of yoghurt for some lovely fruity dipping.

❼ Do a haiku or two

You can write a haiku about anything really, but traditionally they're supposed to be simple observations of nature.

Observe a bit of nature and 5-7-5 it – that's the number of syllables, remember? Here's one ...

Six-spot ladybird
Climbing up a green grass stem
Nearly at the top

Here's another ...

A blue summer sky
Little clouds drifting slowly
High above the earth

❽ Slow down with a sloth

A sloth is the ultimate chilled-out animal. It moves so slowly that a sort of green algae grows on it. Find out some sloth-facts from books or websites and download a picture for your wall. Take your time! Let your sloth inspire you to slow down.

❾ Adopt a plant

Beg, borrow or buy a houseplant. It'll look nice, make the air fresher and bring a little piece of nature right into your room. If you keep it for a while, you'll be able to notice it growing – nothing dramatic, just in its own sweet time.

⑩ Switch off for a day

Have one day screen-free – no TV or computer or playing games on your mobile.

Tip: If you're a sociable sort, get your family or friends to join in – then you can all put your heads together and come up with something different to do.

3 WEDNESDAY

Let your hair down

Sometimes you can get stressed out worrying about what other people think. You might feel worried in case people laugh at you, which is fear of embarrassment, or worried they might reject you, which is more about peer and parental pressure.

Oooh ... Embarrassing!

Suppose you say or do the wrong thing? Suppose you get the wrong end of the stick? Suppose you trip over or drop the catch or find out that your zip's been open since breaktime?

Cringe!

One of the great things about being on holiday is that nobody knows you. If something embarrassing happens and everyone looks, who cares? You'll never see any of those people again. That's why your dad is happy to wear his pink coconuts-and-monkeys shirt on the beach in

Spain, though he wouldn't be seen dead in it in his normal life. It's why you don't have to curl up and die when you're walking along the beach beside him.

No one likes feeling embarrassed but some people handle it much better than others and that means they don't stress about it. Do the 'Laugh, hide … or die?' quiz and see if fear of something embarrassing happening could be causing you stress.

Laugh, hide … or die?

What would you do if …

1 You did a loud fart in
   assembly   ☐   ☐   ☐
                   laugh hide die

2 Everyone found out
   about your secret crush   ☐   ☐   ☐
                   laugh hide die

3 Your mum picked you up
   from school with her
   new boyf, the   ☐   ☐   ☐
   woolly mammoth   *laugh hide die*

4 You gave the wrong
answer in class and
everyone laughed   ☐ ☐ ☐
laugh hide die

5 You had to wear odd socks
because all the others
were in the wash   ☐ ☐ ☐
laugh hide die

6 You were showing off
your skateboarding skills
and fell off   ☐ ☐ ☐
laugh hide die

7 You were grumbling about
your bossy-boots teacher ...
and he was standing
right behind you!   ☐ ☐ ☐
laugh hide die

8 You choked on your
cheese sandwich and
everyone got sprayed   ☐ ☐ ☐
laugh hide die

9 You splashed water down
your front so it looked
like you'd wet yourself   ☐ ☐ ☐
laugh hide die

10 You woke up with a big
spot on your chin   ☐ ☐ ☐
laugh hide die

Totals ☐ ☐ ☐

Results

Mostly laugh   You've got no problem with embarrassment plus you're great fun to be around.

Mostly hide   By getting upset you draw attention to yourself just when you don't want it – that's twice the cringe. No wonder you worry!

Mostly die   Your fatal fear of embarrassment could be seriously stressing you out.

Here's a three-point plan for handling mortifying moments –

1   *Be realistic*

Everyone makes mistakes or looks silly sometimes – that's just a fact of life.

2   *Have a sense of proportion*

People laughing at you isn't the end of the world – no one ever really died from embarrassment.

3   *Lighten up!*

Seeing the funny side means you get to enjoy the joke as well. It isn't always easy and sometimes you can only do it later on, looking back, but it's a good goal to have in mind and some of the Wednesday mini-breaks will give you techniques for achieving it.

Peer and parental pressure

Trying to fit in with what other people want you to be can be a big stress, especially if it's at odds with what you want for yourself. Maybe your mum wants you to get great marks at school and go to university, because she never had a chance to go herself. Fine if that's what you want too, but pretty stressy if you find schoolwork difficult, and want to stop doing tests and essays as soon as possible.

53

Maybe your dad wants you to be a sporting superstar but you're starting to feel bored with your training routine and wanting to take up surfboarding instead.

Then there's peer pressure – you know how that goes. Having to have the right clothes and stuff so you don't look like a saddo; having to be interested in the right things.

Tressa

Tressa had been friends with De-Anne, Sasha and Martha since they were in the infants' class and they had always hung out together. But when the other three suddenly got into boys and clothes, Tressa started to feel left out.

She didn't want to stop being friends so she joined in with all the mushy movies, magazines and makeover days. She pretended that she loved shopping and trying things on – she even pretended she had a crush.

But all the time, she felt like a fraud. What if they found out that she secretly wished they were still hanging out at the park and making a mess and watching silly-kid-films?

Tressa got doubly stressed because she couldn't relax in ways she wanted to, plus she was worried that there must be something wrong with her because she didn't like the same things as her friends.

It's bad enough having to try to fit in with your friends' style and interests but it can get even more stressful trying to go along with how they behave. Supposing you're in a group that likes teasing younger kids? Supposing they want to go shop-lifting or bunk off school?

Sometimes you may have to make a stand.

Justine

Justine's mate, Tammy, started smoking and soon everyone in the group had tried it too. Justine was the only one who refused to join in.

She didn't criticise them for smoking and she didn't try to make them stop – so why did they keep going on at her about it? At first she felt confused, then she felt hurt, then she felt angry. She absolutely wasn't going to let them pressure her!

When they saw that she wasn't going to budge, they stopped nagging and teasing – and pretty soon some of them stopped smoking too.

Here's a three-point plan to help you get a handle on peer and parental pressure –

1   *Be true to yourself*

Don't let go of your secret dreams for yourself even if you can't get other people to take them seriously, and don't ever do something you feel is wrong just because your mates are doing it.

2   *Do your own thing whenever you can*

Sometimes you have to compromise in order to fit in, but you aren't with your mates 24:7 – ditto your parents – so use your 'you' time to explore the things you're really interested in.

3   *Accept and enjoy the fact that everyone's different*

It's easier to feel free to be yourself if you let other people feel free too.

Unless you decide to become a hermit, you're bound to feel social pressure from time to time and worry about making a fool of yourself or not fitting in. But you don't have to get stressed out about it.

You can learn to handle embarrassment and take time out from other people's expectations.

Get some 'you' time right now by choosing a Wednesday mini-break.

Menu of Wednesday mini-breaks

❶ Family funnies

Funny stories are part of every family's history – memories you can all share and enjoy.

'Do you remember the first time the Thompsons came to tea? Mum gave Dad a plate of spaghetti and it all slipped off into his lap!'

'Yeah, and what about when little Joe swallowed the marble and made us all look in his potty when it came out the other end?!'

Think of three family funnies and ask yourself, could they have been embarrassing at the time they happened?

❷ Turn cringe to comedy

Think of something really embarrassing that happened to you – something that still makes you cringe.

Close your eyes and imagine you can see a television set. Switch it on. The programme is a comedy, and it's the story of your cringe-y moment. Watch the scene unfold and hear the audience laughter. Can you join in?

❸ Go for it!

Sometimes, you probably play it safe by avoiding doing things that might turn out to be embarrassing, such as reading your work out in front of the class or answering a question when you aren't a hundred per cent sure you'll get it right. Or holding the door for your teacher – your mates might laugh at you and call you a creep. Or playing a different position – you might be hopeless and let lots of goals in.

Watch out for one of those times today – but instead of drawing back, go for it. Even if an opportunity doesn't arise, feel how great it is to know that fear of being embarrassed isn't going to stop you doing anything.

❹ 'So embarrassing!'

Write the story of something embarrassing that happened to you, as if it happened to someone else. So instead of saying 'I had too much wedding cake and threw up – actually at the table ...' use 'she' or 'he.'

Make it funny – exaggerate or change the details if you like. 'She had fifteen pieces of cake and then threw up all over her sister's wedding dress!'

Imagining it happened to someone else can really help you see the funny side.

❺ Your cringe order

Look at this list and put it in cringe order, from 1 to 5, where 1 is the least cringe-y area and 5 the most.

Parents

Schoolwork

Stuff (clothes, mobile, mp3, etc.)

Looks (face and body-shape)

Personality (moody, dizzy, gloomy, etc.)

Simply noticing that you feel more confident in some areas of your life than others can make the tricky stuff feel more manageable.

❻ Be a comedy commentator

Whenever you feel stressed today imagine you're in a film and do a funny commentary.

'His mum says she woke him up but he doesn't believe her ... he's in a *baaaaaad* mood ... He's throwing on his clothes ... He's rushing into the bathroom ... He's turning the tap on really hard ... Who left that empty shampoo bottle in the sink? He's gonna need a new shirt now ...'

Comedy is a way of feeling more detached and not taking things too seriously. This technique is particularly useful for dealing with embarrassing situations.

❼ Make a monster kenning

Write a kenning called 'Me'. A kenning is a poem where each line has two words, the second one ending '-er'. Think of as many things as you can about yourself and make it a monster kenning ...

> Dog owner
> Bully hater
> Story writer
> Pasta eater
> Jeans wearer
> Pool swimmer ...

The better you see yourself the easier it is to be yourself – and that's the best way of resisting pressure from other people.

❽ Fill in the gaps

Fill in the gaps in this sentence – 'I feel happy when ... because ...' Do it three times, thinking of different things if you can.

Then fill in the gaps in your day, doing the things that make you feel happiest.

Doing the things you like means you're being yourself and not worrying about other people's expectations. No stress!

❾ Draw the line

Get a piece of paper and draw a line across the middle. Above the line, make a list of things you do or have done in the past in order to fit in with your friends. Below the line, list the things you would not be willing to do.

Friends can support you in times of stress, but they can also stress you out by putting you under pressure. Knowing where you draw the line helps you feel more secure in yourself.

Watch boring 'Buffy',
pretend I like fantasy stories,
nag Mum and Dad for money to buy
nice trainers

Lie to my mum, smoke, wag school ...

⑩ Be your hero

Who's your greatest hero? Take the first person that comes into your head – it might be your fave footie star, Harry Potter, your mum or dad ...

Close your eyes and imagine being your hero. Take your time. Go through a whole day, from getting out of bed to going to sleep at night. Where are you? What are you doing? How are you feeling? What are the people around you saying?

This doesn't only feel good – it shows you your secret dreams for yourself, and helps you stay focused on them and not be pressurised by other people.

4 THURSDAY

Have a laugh

Five hundred years ago, a v. famous French doctor called Francois Rabelais said 'Laughter is the best medicine' (or words to that effect) – and now modern science is proving he was right! New research shows that the best cure for stress is laughter and in fact, having a good laugh turns out to have loads of other health benefits too. For example:

● It boosts your immune system so you're less likely to catch infections.

- It helps your breathing, which is great for people with asthma.

- It improves your circulation, keeping your heart healthy and your brain well supplied with oxygen.

- It can provide effective pain relief (if you don't believe this, do your own bit of medical research next time you've got a headache or tummyache, and try watching or reading something hilarious).

Laughing is so good for you that doctors are prescribing laughter therapy for stress-related illnesses and there are laughter clinics run by the National Health Service. This is true!

When it comes to stress-busting, laughter works in five fantastic ways –

1 Laughing makes your body produce lower levels of stress-hormones (that's cortisol, dopac, adrenaline and growth hormone, for all you boffins) and release more feel-good chemicals (endorphins).

2 When you laugh, your pulse quickens and your blood-pressure rises – then when you stop, they settle down to a lower rate than before you got the giggles. That means you're more relaxed after a good laugh than you were before.

3 A good belly-laugh can exercise every muscle in your body – all 400 of them – and that means when you've finished laughing every muscle in your body feels completely relaxed.

4 Laughing gives you a break from worrying about things, because it's a scientific fact that you can't fret and chortle at the same time.

5 The stress-busting effects of having a laugh can last for 12-24 hours.

Laughter is one of our natural defences against stress, and we use it automatically to defuse stressful situations. You might notice this when you share things you feel upset about with your mates, like Jackson did.

Jackson

Jackson had a big row with his dad and by the time he got to school he was still fuming. 'All I did was get out of bed two minutes late. I mean – what is his problem?'

Jackson's mates straight away laughed and joined in. Shayne said, 'My mum goes mental if I do that ...' 'I get the cold flannel treatment,' goes Dean. Andy topped them all with his smelly old dog being let in to lick his face. Dog breath first thing in the morning – yuk!

As they went on swapping horror stories, even Jackson saw the funny side and his bad temper went away.

A little laughter every day isn't just good for making you feel less stressed – it will stop you from getting stressed in the first place. So how do you know if you're getting enough laughter in your life? There's no need to dash off to the doc's – you can check your laughter levels by doing this quick questionnaire.

Do you need more laughter in your life?

A When was the last time you saw something funny on TV?

1 Last night.

2 In the last week.

3 I only watch news and documentaries.

B What do you most like doing with your mates?

1 Playing sports and games.

2 Larking around.

3 Having political debates.

C What do your family chats mostly consist of?

1 Grumbling competitions.

2 Catching up with each other's news.

3 Having a giggle.

D Where can you find giant snails?

1 I don't know – I'm not very good at biology.

2 Hold on … I know this one … Doh! You'll have to tell me.

3 At the end of giants' fingers!

Scores   A 1=3, 2=2, 3=0

B 1=2, 2=3, 3=1

C 1=0, 2=2, 3=3

D 1=1, 2=2, 3=3

Results

10-12 points   You're getting loads of laughs. Keep up the good work!

5-9 points   Not bad, but you could think of upping your daily dose.

Less than 5   You need an emergency transfusion! Here it comes ...

*Doctor, doctor – I get
a pain in my eye
every time I drink tea.*

Try taking the spoon out!

Be your own laughter therapist

You don't need a doc to arrange some laughter therapy for you – you can do it for yourself.

Laughter therapy has no unwanted side-effects plus it's

- Fun

- Free

- Sociable – smiley people are great to be with.

- Safe – unless you laugh your head off, of course (ha ha … boing!).

So lighten up! Take time out from the serious side of life and book yourself a mini-break at the stress-buster laughter clinic.

Menu of Thursday mini-breaks

❶ Watch a funny film

If your family likes watching comedies you've probably got some favourites on video or DVD at home. Simply thinking about watching a funny film makes your body start producing happy chemicals, so you can get the stress-busting benefits for hours before you even switch it on. (This has been scientifically proven – seriously!)

If you haven't got any comedy films, find someone who can lend you one. Maybe they'd like to watch it with you? That would be double the fun.

❷ Post a joke

Think of a joke. Write it out. Get some Blu-Tack and stick it on a wall! The chances are, next time you look someone else will have posted a joke too.

I did this when I was a kid and pretty soon our loo wall was covered in jokes.

If you prefer, send a joke to all your mates in MSN, or get your teacher to give you a bit of display space and start a class joke board.

❸ Have a smiletastic day!

Draw a little smiley on your thumbnail and every time you see it, smile!

When you smile, even if you don't feel particularly happy or amused, the movement of your face muscles sends a message to your brain to start releasing happy hormones.

Plus, it connects you with other people, and they smile back – so you're spreading the stress-busting around. Nice!

Smile alert! Better send out some happy hormones.

❹ Do the wacky wordsearch

There are 12 funny things hidden in the grid, written either across or down. Think about each one as you search for it, and crack a smile!

I've done one to get you started.

custard pie, joke, jest, limerick, pun, laughter,

chuckle, giggle, fun, smiley, grin, chortle

S	C	H	O	R	T	L	E	B	S
F	U	N	P	L	W	A	L	N	M
I	S	O	N	A	V	M	U	S	I
D	T	C	H	U	C	K	L	E	L
Y	A	X	O	G	I	G	G	L	E
K	R	E	J	H	U	R	D	J	Y
A	D	Z	B	T	O	I	J	E	P
N	P	U	N	E	Q	N	O	S	V
L	I	M	E	R	I	C	K	T	E
O	E	C	V	W	N	P	E	Z	D

❺ Best-ever sitcom moments

Write down your three favourite sitcoms or cartoons. Choose one, and write down the three funniest moments in the series. That should bring a smile to your face!

If you can't think of three funny moments, watch some episodes to remind yourself.

❻ Hang out with someone who makes you laugh

Make a positive decision to keep clear of gloomies and hang out with your most fun-loving friends.

Be a fun-loving friend today as well – if you feel a touch of the grumps coming on, don't go there! For one fun Thursday try to keep it light, one hundred per cent.

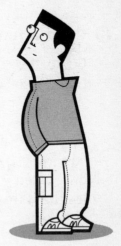

❼ Play a funny game

Think of a board game / computer game / outdoors game like hide-and-seek / family game like charades – anything that always makes you laugh.

Get a few friends round or rope in your family, and play it.

Note: If you can't think of any, ask your mates what games give them the giggles and get them to show you how to play.

❽ Read a funny book

Go to the school library and look through the books – you can tell the funny ones by the covers.

If you see one you fancy, give it a test-drive by reading the first two pages. If it hasn't made you smile by then, put it back and try another one. When you find one that does it for you, take it out. Have half an hour of chuckles reading it after school.

➒ Make a mad picture

You'll need a piece of paper, a few mags, some scissors and a glue stick.

Cut out some pics you like – and put them together in unlikely combinations. You could have a girl with a flower instead of a head, or a dog with a cucumber for a tail, or a seascape with things floating on the water, such as a fridge, an elephant, a car ...

Note: If you prefer, and you've got the right software, you can do the same sort of thing on the computer.

➓ Do a laughter work-out

This is based on a form of exercise called 'laughter yoga' (yes, really!).

Take a deep breath in through your nose, pushing your tummy out and then your chest as well, so that your lungs fill with air from the bottom up. Hold the breath for a few seconds and then sigh it out slowly through your mouth.

On the next breath, instead of sighing the air out, laugh it out. Keep laughing until all the air has gone and then fill up again. Repeat this for five breaths, counting them off on your fingers, working up from a chuckle to a belly-laugh.

Note: It might help if you think of something funny before you start, but you don't have to.

5 FRIDAY

Pamper yourself

Pampering yourself is about pleasing your senses, and pleasure is a super stress-buster. When you touch, see, hear, smell or taste something nice, your brain starts pumping out feel-good chemicals and stops producing so many stressy ones.

It's a natural instinct to reach for some sort of physical comforter when you feel stressed. Babies suck their thumbs or cry for their dummy; small children want their teddy or blanket or special toy.

As you get older you may turn on some music to calm yourself down, or eat some chocolate, or have a cup of tea.

All comforters can be addictive, so although a little bit of what you fancy really does do you good, a lot of what you fancy really doesn't.

Though you've probably got your own favourite stress-busting comforters, the best pampering comes from pleasing your senses in lots of different ways.

Pleasure good – pain bad!

There are five senses and each one can bring experiences of pleasure and pain. You can keep your general stress levels down by simply seeking out pleasurable experiences and avoiding unpleasant ones as far as possible. (Obviously, you can't avoid pain completely because this is real life.)

See how good you are at making feel-good choices by doing the 'stress-to-less-stress maze'.

The stress-to-less-stress maze

Start in the middle and try to find the best de-stress way out. Every time you have a choice, take a moment to really imagine the smells, sights, sounds, tastes and feelings before you decide which way to go. Keep a count of every time you get an 'ouch!'

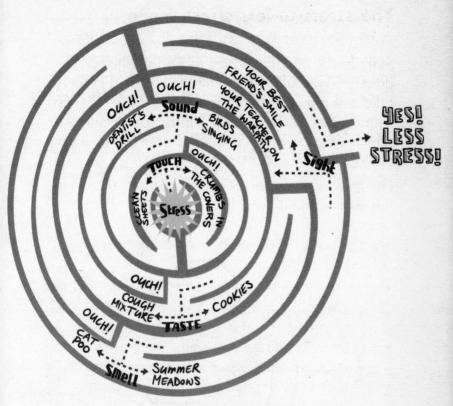

YES! LESS STRESS!

Results

No ouches – what a sensible person you are!

Any ouches at all – you're having a laugh!

The stress-to-less-stress maze is easy because it's easy in life to make pleasurable choices once you begin to notice and think about it. So next time you're tempted to take the short cut to school alongside the sewage treatment works, think what holding your nose for five minutes is doing to your stress levels and leave time to go the long way round down Leafy Lane instead!

The trick is to notice when your senses are jarred and sort it, like Emily did.

Emily

Emily's mum forgot she had promised to give her a lift to school and now Emily would have to walk. She crashed through the bathroom, flung some bread in the toaster and started to throw things into her school bag.

By the time she had finished, her toast was burnt. She bit off a sooty corner – yuk! – and just at that moment her big bro walked in. Seeing her standing there with her tongue out, he burst out laughing, and then she did too, pebble-dashing the table with black crumbs.

Emily didn't want to stay in a stressy mood, so she offered the burnt toast to her bro and grabbed a fresh piece of bread as she headed for the door. That tasted better.

She'd only gone a few yards down the road when she noticed she had a bit of grit in her shoe. She could have hobbled on, but she decided to stop and shake it out. That felt better.

Emily strode along, eyes down, looking at the pavement. Squashed chewing-gum, bird droppings, cigarette ends ... She could have gone all the way to school like that but she decided to look around her instead. Flowers in gardens, smiley people, scudding clouds ... That looked better.

She could have gone along the High Street but she knew there were road works with men drilling a trench, so she decided to stay on the side street for an extra block instead. Birds singing, bees buzzing ... That sounded better.

She got to school as the bell went. She could have gone through the nearest side entrance past the toilets but she decided to go in the main door instead – that smelt better.

Emily still felt a bit stressed but it would have been much worse if she'd arrived with a tummy full of burnt toast, a sore foot, a picture of pavement in her head, the ringing of road drills in her ears and the smell of the toilets in her nose.

So keep your stress levels down by soothing your senses. Start now by going to the stress-buster health spa and choosing your Friday mini-break.

Menu of Friday mini-breaks

❶ Your pleasure profile

Pleasure is personal and one person's great stress-buster can be another person's stress-maker ...

List the five senses – touch, taste, smell, sight, hearing – and think of three things for each that you find pleasurable and three that you don't like at all.

Being aware of what gives you pleasure helps you to get more of it in your life.

❷ Tickle your taste buds

Have a dig around in your kitchen cupboards and create a taste-bud-tickling snack including:

- Something sweet – for example, a few raisins or cake decorations.

- Something salty – for example a few peanuts or crisps.

- Something fruity – such as fruit!

- Something smooth – for example, a bit of cheese.

- Something crunchy – for example a cracker.

- Anything else you find that you fancy.

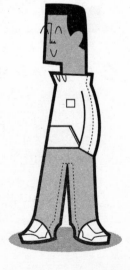

Note: Check with your mum or dad before you start.

Another note: Tidy up any spills and close any packets!

❸ Go to the beach!

Lie down on your bed and shut your eyes. Imagine you're walking along a beach. The sand is fine and white, and the sea is sparkly and blue. Lie down on the warm sand, close your eyes and enjoy the warmth of the sun on your skin.

Listen to the sea lapping against the shore and the gulls crying high above you.

Taste the salt on your lips. Breathe in the fresh sea air.

Whenever you feel stressed you can use the power of your imagination to feel pleasurable sensations and get those happy hormones flowing.

❹ Make a feely A-Z

Do an A-Z of things that feel, smell, taste, sound or look good to you – A is for apple juice, B is for banana sandwiches, C is for my cat's fur, D is for Dad's bristly chin ...

If you can't think of anything for one letter, move on to the next and go back at the end. Pause to imagine each one. Enjoy!

Note: X is tricky so if you don't like the sound of xylophones you can cheat and have something xtra fluffy or xitingly bright or xtraordinarily tuneful.

❺ Do a colour test

Different colours affect your mood in different ways. Blue has a calming effect, which is probably why most school uniforms are blue – they don't want you leaping around in lessons!

Test what effects colours have on you by choosing three different tops from your wardrobe and wearing each one for half an hour.

Clock the best stress-buster and whip it on next time your mum gets in a strop.

❻ Make a mix-up poem

For some feely fun, draw three columns under the headings 'sense', 'thing' and 'something about it'. Look around and record the things you can see, smell, taste, touch and hear around you.

Sense	Thing	Something about it
Hear	my computer whirring	under the desk
See	a thrush	eating a worm
Touch	a green plastic pig	full of paper clips
Smell	vanilla soap	that I washed my hands with
Taste	three brazil nuts	from the rainforest

Now mix them up and make a poem!

*I can hear three brazil nuts eating a worm
I can see a green plastic pig from the
rainforest ...*

❼ Kick back with cool tunes

Give yourself half an hour listening to music you enjoy. If you find it hard just listening, occupy your hands and eyes by doing a bit of doodling while you listen. Use several different pens or pencils and just let them do what they like.

Don't even try to make a great picture – the idea is just to enjoy the colours and shapes as they appear on the page.

⑧ Go on a smell quest

Smells can be so subtle that a lot of the time we hardly even notice them – except your baby bro's nappies, of course.

Make this whole day a smell quest. Notice as many smells as you can – in your house, out of doors, at school. At the end of the day, think back and write down all the smells you can remember. Put a star beside the ones you really liked, then you'll be more aware of enjoying them next time.

⑨ When you were little ...

What was your best stress-buster when you were little? Maybe you had a special cuddly or a sucky-ribbon, or a blanket or pillow you liked to carry round. Maybe you sucked your thumb.

Close your eyes and think about all the ways your comforter soothed your senses. Notice what happens in your body as you do this.

⑩ **Look through your fingers**

Find ten items made of different fabrics – a woolly sweater, a silky jim-jams top, a face flannel, some denims ...

Shut your eyes and 'see' each one with your fingers. Lift it up and feel it against your cheek. How would you describe it – smooth or rough, warm or cool, thick or flimsy?

Noticing your physical connection to everyday things helps to calm you and stop stressful thoughts.

6 SATURDAY

Get physical

When you've had a hard day the last thing you feel like doing is getting some exercise. Say you didn't understand what you were supposed to be doing in class, and then your mates were being off with you at breaktime and then your after-school club was boring ... and when you finally got home your mum and dad were having a row … What you'd probably want to do is shut yourself in your bedroom and turn the TV up.

But physical exercise is a much better stress-buster. After a tough day there's nothing like practising your ball skills, or shooting some hoops, going for a swim or having a bike ride, or taking the dog for a walk (it'll help him to de-stress as well).

Exercise isn't just a great emergency stress-buster – it also helps prevent stress building up in the first place. Getting physical makes you fitter, and fitness acts as a buffer against stress.

So how come most of us choose this ...

instead of these ...

Because it's easier!

Maybe on holidays we're happy to have long hikes and bike rides, go swimming and play cricket on the beach from dawn to dusk, but for all the rest of the year at home it's just too easy to slip into lazy habits and hibernate on the settee.

See if laziness could be a problem you need to shake by doing the 'Are you a couch potato or a spring bean?' quiz. (If you can't be bothered to do the quiz, you're probably a potato!)

Are you a couch potato or a spring bean?

1. You're watching a dull DVD with your mates and you want some munch to relieve the boredom. Do you

A. Go and get a snack.

B. Forget the TV and the snack and do something else.

C. Wait for someone else to get up and ask them to get you a snack.

2. You live quite close to school so you can choose whether to walk or take the bus. Do you

A. Mix and match, depending on the weather.

B. Always walk and enjoy the exercise.

C. Always take the bus – it's more hassle but less tiring.

3. Your bedroom's in the basement and the loo's two storeys up. Do you

A. Go when you have to.

B. Never even notice those two flights of stairs.

C. Cross your legs and put it off till you can't bear the pain.

4. It's a family day out at the beach. Do you prefer to

A. Find a spot to put your towel down near the entrance.

B. Walk along a bit and spread yourselves out where there's more space.

C. Picnic in the car park.

5. Some of your mates have signed up for Saturday kick-boxing sessions and you'd quite like to go. Do you

A. Join in.

B. Join in and also suggest a quick swim afterwards since there's a public pool next to the sports centre.

C. Not bother – Saturday mornings were invented for lying in.

	A	B	C
Question 1	☐	☐	☐
2	☐	☐	☐
3	☐	☐	☐
4	☐	☐	☐
5	☐	☐	☐

Results

Mostly A   You're not a spring bean or a couch potato – you're a happy medium, and that's good enough exercise-wise

Mostly B   You're a spring bean – even better!

Mostly C   You're a couch potato – better get up off your behind before you start to put down roots!

If you're a couch potato, you're probably thinking 'The trouble is I'm just not sporty!' But just because you don't enjoy sport at school, don't assume that means you can't enjoy any sports at all. Most school sport involves teams and competition – and getting changed into embarrassing shorts in front of lots of people who you maybe don't get on with.

However, there are loads of different kinds of sport that schools can't offer, and you might find you can be really sporty outside school, like Aaron did.

Aaron

Aaron was quite good at football but he didn't really enjoy it. The problem was that he was heavier than most of the other boys, and every time he changed into his football kit he worried that they might tease him. He was also quite good at athletics, but that was even worse because the girls were out on the playing-field too. Aaron wished he could give up doing sports at all. 'I'm just not sporty,' he thought.

But then he heard his uncle talking to his dad about the new archery club at his local sports centre. It sounded good. He decided to give it a go.

You don't have to wear shorts to shoot an arrow – that was the first great thing about it – plus you don't often get a chance to hang out with your cool uncle. When Aaron lined up for the target, pulled back the bow, let the arrow fly, it was such a fantastic feeling! Aaron found he was a sports-lover after all.

The key to success in sport is the same as the key to success in everything else – enjoyment. You need to find something that fits your personality. Supposing you're a very sociable sort, then long-distance running isn't going to be for you. Hours out training on your own ... no way!

 If you're sociable, you might want to find a team game – but what if you don't like competition, and you find it stressful to have everyone in the team relying on you not to make a mistake? Then you'd be happier with a sport that you could do with some mates in a non-competitive way, like ice-skating, for example, or an hour a week messing around at the pool.

There are all kinds of sports to suit all kinds of people and it's worth trying to find one that suits you because –

1   All sports involve getting active, and doing a session once or twice a week makes you take a more active attitude to life in general.

2   Being more active boosts your general health and that means your body can cope better with stress.

3 Doing a sport you enjoy makes you feel better about yourself – this has been scientifically proven! And feeling good is a great buffer against stress because when you like yourself, little things are less likely to bother you.

4 Sports give you time out from day-to-day stresses like schoolwork and family tensions.

Taking up a sport is a tip-top way to start having a more active lifestyle but if you absolutely hate the idea, there's no need to. You don't have to run marathons and play in leagues in order to get fitter. You can bump up your fitness by simply running up and down stairs a few extra times a day or getting off the bus a stop early.

So get down to the stress-buster gym and check out the Saturday mini-breaks. Some are sporty and some aren't, but they all come packed with stress-busting goodness!

Menu of Saturday mini-breaks

❶ Do some disco dancing

Saturday night is disco night, but you don't have to find an actual disco or show yourself up on the dance floor – just shut your bedroom door, put on your fave CD, pick up your hairbrush microphone and go for it!

If you're feeling sociable, ask some mates round and work out your own dance routine or, if you've got a dance mat, do some disco dancing on that.

❷ Get on your bike

Write a list of all the friends and rellies who live within cycling distance of your house. Choose one and cycle over to see them.

If you haven't got a bike, go on your roller blades, jog or walk.

❸ Check out your local sports centre

You might be surprised by how many fun activities are on offer at your local sports centre. Pick up some leaflets and check the notice-boards.

If it's not too far, walk down there – but if it is, get your mum or dad to take you. Failing that, have a look at the sports centre's website.

See if there's anything you'd like to sign up for.

❹ Take the stairs

Not literally – that would be good for your fitness but bad for everyone else who needs to get to an upper floor!

Going up and down stairs is top exercise, so make friends with the stairs at home.

Every time you have to go up or down today, do it twice for luck!

❺ Think yourself fit

Scientists recently discovered a very interesting thing – simply imagining yourself doing some exercise from the comfort of your armchair can be a fitness boost!

Sit somewhere you won't be disturbed for ten minutes, take a few deep breaths to get in the mood, and start imagining!

Choose any sport that appeals to you, and do a whole session, starting with warming-up and ending with warming-down. Feel what happens to your heart-rate, body temperature and muscle tone – that's happening for real, not just in your imagination.

⑥ Play shipwrecked

This is one of my favourite games – it's fast and funny, and you can play it anywhere with your family or friends. You need at least four people, but the more the merrier.

The idea is, your ship's been wrecked and everyone's overboard, swimming around among the wreckage. There aren't enough pieces of wreckage for everyone to climb up on, so one person is always in the water – and so is the big bad man-eating shark (otherwise known as 'it').

You can choose anything to be your bits of wreckage – a railing to hold on to, a stained paving-stone, a step ... The shark can't get you on a piece of wreckage, but there's only room for one person on each piece, so if someone else jumps onto your piece you have to run to another one. If the shark gets you on the way, he has to run because now you're the shark.

The game ends when everyone's worn out.

❼ Your perfect sport

Write down three things about yourself, the first three that come to mind, for example, 'artistic, cheerful, sociable', 'serious, bit of a loner, nature-lover', 'competitive, energetic, impulsive' ...

Now think of as many sports as you can that fit your character profile. For example, if you're artistic, cheerful and sociable, you might like some sort of dance, roller disco or even synchronised swimming; if you're serious, solitary and nature-loving, how about yoga, tai chi, walking and jogging? If you're competitive, energetic and impulsive, some sort of team game could be good – how many can you think of?

❽ Get your brain into gear

If you think you aren't sporty that attitude could hold you back from exploring your sporting potential. Get rid of it with a bit of gentle brain-washing!

Tie a piece of coloured thread around your shirt button or watch strap or shoelace as a memory-jogger and every time you notice it say to yourself, 'Right now, I'm a really fit and sporty person!' It may feel ridiculous but it works. Strange but true.

❾ Walk and talk

Instead of lounging about chatting to your mates on the phone, walk around as you talk – unless, of course, the receiver's on one of those wiggly wires.

If you hang out with your mates, instead of just sitting around with them, have a walk as you talk.

❿ Get sporty

Do a half hour session of any physical activity you like, for example, swimming, walking, biking, skate-boarding, football, rounders, skipping, jogging, keep fit, dance mat, table-tennis, frisbee ...

7 SUNDAY

A change is as good as a rest

The little things in life can really stress you out – your brother walking into your bedroom like he owns it, your mate banging on about her latest crush, your mum buying the wrong biscuits ... It can drive you mad.

Going on holiday is a good stress-buster because it gets you away from your normal life, so all the annoying things that can feel so huge disappear in the distance, the way your house does as you drive away.

As well as giving you a different perspective on your normal life, going on holiday also means you have lots of new things to take your mind off the ones that usually bug you.

But you don't have to go to Brazil or the Bahamas to get the stress-busting benefits of having a holiday. Every time you try something new it's like a little holiday from your normal life.

It's easy to get stuck in a rut – just doing the same things every day and never trying anything new – and the more stuck you are the more stressful it feels when something upsets your routine. That's when you need to ring the changes!

Do the changes check-list and find out if you could be stuck in a rut.

The changes check-list

When was the last time you	In the last month	In the last 6 months	More than 6 months ago / can't remember
1 Tried a new game	☐	☐	☐
2 Had a new hairstyle	☐	☐	☐
3 Ate something you'd never tasted before	☐	☐	☐
4 Went somewhere you'd never been before	☐	☐	☐

	In the last month	In the last 6 months	More than 6 months ago / can't remember
5 Asked someone new over	☐	☐	☐
6 Changed your bedroom round	☐	☐	☐
7 Learnt how to do something new	☐	☐	☐
8 Read a book by a new author	☐	☐	☐
9 Did something different at break time	☐	☐	☐
10 Watched the sort of TV show you wouldn't normally watch	☐	☐	☐

Results

5+ in the last month – Excellent! You're too busy trying new things to stress over trifles.

5+ in the last 6 months – You're a bit set in your ways, so new things could feel stressful.

5+ more than 6 months ago – Watch out! The walls are closing in ...

Choosing to try new things is a non-stressful way of making changes because it's up to you what you do – you're in control. If you do it lots it doesn't only take your mind off little things that might annoy you, it also helps you deal with big things when they come along.

Big changes – no stress!

Little changes you choose are as good as a rest, but big ones can be stressful – for example, moving house, going to a new school, getting a new baby sister.

If you're used to living adventurously you get lots of practice at handling new things and that means when something big happens, you can take it in your stride, no stress.

The same goes for all those little unexpected changes life can throw at you, such as last-minute changes of plan.

Lottie and Belle

Lottie and her twin sister Belle always went to see a panto with their cousins at Christmas and they were really looking forward to it. But then their Auntie phoned to say she hadn't been able to get any tickets so there would have to be a change of plan. 'How about going to see a ballet instead?' she suggested.

Neither Lottie nor Belle had ever seen a ballet before but they reacted very differently. Lottie got upset because she had her heart set on going to the panto and she wasn't sure if she would like the ballet. She worried about whether to go or not.

Belle was disappointed too but being a more adventurous type, she had discovered that sometimes when you try something new, even if it doesn't seem very interesting at first, you can have a lovely surprise – and she didn't stress about it at all.

So live adventurously – try lots of new things – have a change from whatever you usually do because a change is as good as a rest. Start right now by choosing a Sunday safari.

Selection of Sunday safaris

❶ Try something you've never eaten before

Yep – it really is as easy as that! You could buy a different snack bar or put mayonnaise on your chips at tea-time instead of ketchup.

Alternatively, you could try mixing familiar foods in new combinations – how about putting some sultanas in your cheese sandwich or a dollop of chocolate mousse on your muesli? Yum!

❷ Get a new bedroom

Obviously, I don't mean turf your big bro out of his lovely big room and move your stuff in. You can get a new room much more easily (and safely, if your big bro's got a temper on him) by simply shifting your furniture around.

Note: It's probably a good idea to tell your parents what you're doing – they might even give you a hand.

❸ Find undiscovered areas

How well do you know your local area? Chances are there are streets really close by that you've never even been down (or footpaths, if you live in the middle of nowhere).

Get a street map of your neighbourhood and mark the roads you know. All the ones you don't know are just waiting for you to discover them.

Note: Don't actually go exploring without checking with your mum or dad first.

Another note: If you haven't got a map of your neighbourhood, you can download one from www.streetmap.co.uk

❹ Send yourself a postcard

Think of somewhere you've never been that you'd really like to go to. For me, that would be Greenland.

Take a piece of paper or card and draw a picture of the place as you imagine it would be.

Turn your picture over and write a message to yourself as if you were really there. 'Hi Jen. It's like the inside of a freezer up here, only colder. I saw a polar bear today ...'

In your imagination, you can travel anywhere and have all kinds of adventures.

❺ Have a change of scene

Do something you normally do in a place you wouldn't normally do it – for example, eat your brekkie in the garden, read your book in the bath, watch TV in your parents' room (check with them first, obviously), do your homework in the kitchen ...

❻ Be a tourist

Look up your local area online or visit your nearest tourist information centre and pick up a bunch of leaflets.

Find some places of interest or attractions you haven't been to. Talk to your mum and dad about going to one, or try to organise an outing with some friends.

Even if you can't go straight away, simply being aware of what's out there makes it much more likely that you'll do it one day.

❼ Programme your brain

Write down these five powerful words –

'I love having new experiences'

Say them five times to yourself and notice how they make you feel. Repeat them whenever you think of it throughout the day and five times again before you go to bed.

Your brain is very suggestible! Even if you don't believe them, saying powerful words like these – which is called making affirmations – will have an effect on how you think about yourself.

❽ All-change yourself!

How do you see yourself? Quiet? Sporty? Funny? Serious? Think about it for a few moments and then draw a pic of yourself. Surround yourself  with your special things – for example, if you love reading draw some books, and if you're sporty maybe a tennis racquet or a football or a climbing wall, depending on what particular sports you enjoy.

Now imagine if you were completely the opposite of that picture. If you think you're quiet, imagine you were loud and boisterous. What might a loud version of you enjoy? What might your special objects be then?

Draw a pic of this imaginary you. How does it feel? Enjoy the difference.

⑨ Have a clothes swap

Swap clothes with a mate for one day, just for a laugh. This is a great way of trying out new styles without having to spend any money. Most people play it safe with clothes simply because it costs too much to ring the changes.

Note: Ideally, choose a mate who's about the same size as you!

⑩ Go on a picnic

A picnic is always a change, unless of course you live in a tent. It can be a big family day out or just you and your best mate in the back yard. If it's raining, you can spread your blanket out on the floor and have a picnic indoors.

For a super-stress-busting picnic, try to include as many of the other stress-busting elements as you can – leaving your worries behind, getting back to nature, letting your hair down, having a laugh, delighting your senses and having a run-around.